BUILDING A WALL of PRAYER

BUILDING A WALL of PRAYER

M. BASILEA SCHLINK

KANAAN PUBLICATIONS
Evangelical Sisterhood of Mary
Darmstadt, Germany and Radlett, England

Designed and Produced in England by
Nuprint Ltd, Station Road, Harpenden, Herts AL5 4SE

Contents

Daniel: A Man of Prayer

Prayer means pouring out our hearts to the Father with complete confidence and infinite trust in His fatherly love.

Natural disasters, unprecedented in force, are occurring with growing frequency and assuming frightening, even apocalyptic, proportions. Yet despite these visible signs of divine judgment, there is no limit to man's hatred of God and to his crimes against humanity. Killings, revolts, wars and civil wars keep flaring up in various parts of the world . . .

God is speaking to us through all these events, which are but the preliminaries to a major judgment upon our depraved world. Despite the deep grief it causes God to resort to such measures, He is forced to do so, because there is no other way to make us listen. When calamity follows calamity almost unremittingly and no continent, indeed, hardly any country or area is spared, even the non-religious ask, 'Is God judging us because there is so much sin in the world?'

At a time like this God, who loves us, does not want us to sink in fear and suffering. His Word shows us in what way His help avails for us: 'Call upon me in the day of trouble; I will deliver you' (Psalm 50:15).

God promises to answer us and come to our aid when we call to Him in utmost need. Indeed, through

Christ Jesus He has become our Father. He pays special attention to His children when they are suffering anxiety and distress, for He loves us and bears the pain with us. He watches over every land and nation. And His heart yearns to help us. Therefore, when one blow after the other strikes and we wonder what to do, we can turn to Him. Does not Jesus say in Matthew 7:7, 'Ask, and it will be given you; seek [an answer, for instance], and you will find'?

God's Answer

> *Prayer means looking away from visible things to the invisible God, who rules over all powers and principalities, over the visible and the invisible.*

We find God's answer in a prayer of Holy Scripture uttered during great affliction. It is the prayer of Daniel in chapter 9 — a real gold mine. Although it was familiar to me, I felt as though I had made a new discovery as I came across it again at a time when the daily news reports were especially serious. This prayer not only reveals the nature of God, but it shows us how we can reach His heart with our prayers and receive help for ourselves and our people during a time of crisis.

One evening as I spoke with the Kanaan* family

---

* Located near Darmstadt, Germany, 'Kanaan' is the headquarters of the Evangelical Sisterhood of Mary, an international, interdenominational organization, founded in 1947 within the framework of the German Evangelical (Protestant) Church.

about the critical situation in our country, it was on my heart to say a word about the comfort offered by the Bible and the challenge to whole-hearted intercession. Reading the prayer of Daniel aloud, I adapted it to our present situation. We all felt the prayer to be a source of great strength, and afterwards everyone received a copy [see page 23]. Because Daniel uttered this prayer in a situation similar to our own, it spoke to our hearts. We could identify ourselves with him in the great concern he felt, because today as long ago the future of a nation was in the balance.

Daniel is deeply shaken by the consequences of sin: disaster has come upon his people and further calamities are threatening to descend. In his distress he does something very specific (and God is waiting for us to do the same every time we hear unsettling news reports): Daniel makes an about-turn. He refuses to let such news preoccupy or depress him. Instead he sets his face towards the Lord God. In other words, he turns away from himself and turns to God. Then he begins to pray with a particular attitude of heart which is essential for answered prayer. I was especially struck by this attitude of Daniel, which put me to shame.

'We have sinned . . .'

> *Prayer means lying prostrate before God as a sinner*
> *and saying, 'I am not worthy to be called Your*
> *child' — and then being taken into His loving arms*
> *as one who has received grace.*

Daniel's starting-point is prayer and supplications
with sackcloth and ashes, the phrase 'sackcloth and
ashes' signifying contrition and repentance for his
sins. Daniel faces up to his own sins and confesses
them, thereby identifying with the great sin and guilt
of his people. This heart-attitude is characteristic of
the entire prayer. It pervades his supplications when
he asks God to send help and to avert the impending
calamities. Without the slightest trace of rebellion or
the hint of a 'Why?', he humbles himself beneath
God's chastening, the disaster which has befallen his
people and which continues to threaten them.

Here the secret of answered prayer is revealed.
Daniel accepts the truth about himself and his people.
Acknowledging that 'our' sins are the cause of the
calamity which has befallen them and which still
hangs over them, he prays:

> We have sinned and committed iniquity, we have
> done wickedly and rebelled, even by departing
> from Your precepts and Your judgments . . . O
> Lord, to us belongs shame of face . . . because we
> have sinned against You (Daniel 9:5-8 RAV).

We can only say the same for ourselves and our
people when we examine our consciences to see

where we have turned aside from God's commandments. For instance:

Have I always told the truth?

Have I been greedy? Have I been envious of others, coveting what they have?

Are my relationships to the other sex under God's dominion? Have I kept my marriage pure and holy — even in my thought world?

Do I tolerate the moral filth around me?

Do I condone the killing of unborn human life?

Am I indifferent when Jesus and God the Father are blasphemed?

Have I been rebellious towards God and people — towards my parents or others in authority?

Am I judgmental towards others and living in strife, hatred and bitterness? Am I preventing God from forgiving me because there is someone I haven't forgiven?

Have I slandered others or gossiped about them?

Have I taken unfair advantage of someone or harmed him in any way?

Am I a good steward of my money, health and time — gifts that God has entrusted to me?

Do I rely too much on people? Am I over-attached to them? Am I so afraid of what they will say or do that I dare not call sin by its proper name and sever relations where necessary? Scripture says, 'Have no fellowship with the unfruitful works of darkness, but rather expose them' (Ephesians 5:11 RAV).

If we step into the light of God, our reaction will be like Daniel's: *We — myself included — have sinned, done wrong and failed to live according to the commandments of God.* We will be filled with shame. Then like Daniel we cannot but declare that God is just and righteous in everything He has now allowed us to experience.

Daniel has the courage to pray like this. But how many react differently? When God allows disaster to strike, how many fall into self-pity and despair, blaming the circumstances, people or God Himself? During the affliction that has come upon him and his nation, Daniel has the humility to humble himself beneath this divine judgment. Behind the enemies oppressing his people he sees the hand of God and accepts the truth: *It's my fault, it's our fault, that disaster has come upon us and God has to punish us. My sins are to blame.* Such a courageous and honest confession, such a humble admission of personal and national guilt, reaches the heart of God.

It is vital that we pray in the same way today. Otherwise we will not experience help in our trials; nor can further calamities be averted or mitigated. Confession of sin and repentance are the prerequisites for receiving help. God is waiting for prayers uttered in a spirit of true penitence as we lie before Him: *I, we, have done wrong and sinned against God and our neighbour. I have not loved God above all else. Nor have I loved my neighbour as myself. If someone was hard for me to bear, I held it against him and nursed resentment in my heart instead of forgiving him. I was domineering, arrogant, determined to have my own way instead of being loving.*

Yes, now we need to accept God's verdict upon our personal lives and admit: *I have not humbled myself in the dust before God and man, as Daniel did. I have not humbled myself beneath the sins of others in the awareness that I am just as great a sinner, failing in other respects.* If we were to do so with all our hearts and turn over a new leaf, our prayers would have power and God would hear them.

If only we would begin to repent with 'sackcloth and ashes' in these troubled times, which are characterized by the preliminary judgments of God and the scourge of terrorism, revolts and other crises. God can give grace only to the humble. In this context that means: Only if our prayer for our nation and ourselves is a cry from the depths can God hear us. How vital it is that we pray in the right spirit at this crucial point in history!

We can almost hear God appealing to us, *Pray, yes, pray as My servant Daniel once prayed. I long for you to receive help and an answer to your prayers. So pray with 'sackcloth and ashes' like Daniel, whom I have given you as an example.*

God Is Looking for Priestly, Sacrificial Souls

> *Prayer means being ready to enter into the fellowship of Jesus' sufferings for the sake of the souls for whom we pray.*

Daniel's prayer has yet another characteristic. We read that he prayed 'with fasting'. This means it was a priestly prayer, underlaid with sacrifices. A picture comes to mind of Jesus Christ, our great high priest, who became the sacrificial lamb, yes, 'like a lamb that is led to the slaughter' (Isaiah 53:7). The imagery in this verse is expressive of the depths of His love. It manifests His very nature. As the Lamb of God, He shed His blood to redeem us. Nor is that all. By virtue of His precious blood He has made us kings and priests (Revelation 1:6).

Why was it that Jesus laid Himself upon the altar and sacrificed Himself? — To redeem us from sin and Satan. This is fundamental. But He also wanted to make priests of us who as a 'chosen race', a 'royal priesthood', would 'offer spiritual sacrifices' (1 Peter 2:5-9). And so it is unthinkable that Jesus should be the sacrificial lamb, whereas His disciples, who follow Him and are members of His Body, should not wish to tread the path of sacrifice. Jesus stressed this time and again: *He who does not renounce all that he has . . . he who does not forsake . . . he who loves his father or mother more than Me . . . he who does not deny himself . . . cannot be My disciple.* If our lives are devoid of sacrifices, we do not really belong to Him; we are not true disciples of His.

The greatest thing that Jesus did for us was

accomplished not by His words, nor by His mighty signs and wonders, but by His sacrifice at Calvary. The same principle applies to us. It is true that we should go about the Lord's work, and, indeed, this is what He expects of us. But there is something else He is looking for in our lives — something even more important. We should offer living sacrifices and become a sacrifice ourselves. Scripture says, 'Present your bodies as a living sacrifice, holy and acceptable to God' (Romans 12:1). The world is crying out for sacrificial altars. The blood of the martyrs is the seed of the Church. They offer up their all, prepared to make even the ultimate sacrifice of their lives. As in the days of Sodom and Gomorrah, the Lord is looking for priestly souls who intercede like Abraham (Genesis 18:20-33). Only if He finds such souls, can He hold back His judgment upon a degenerate world. Their prayers are essential for help and renewal to come. However, there must be enough people who give themselves as a sacrifice, practising on a small scale what their Lord did to save the world. Out of love for mankind He sacrificed Himself as a lamb. Thus we, too, are called to make sacrifices, and the Lord will show each of us what our particular sacrifices are to be.

We are living in an era when everything seems to be heading towards ruin and Satan is on the rampage, conquering one stronghold after the other. At such a time our Lord Jesus Christ longs to find sacrificial souls who will join Him in holding back the destructive forces of evil. Power lies in sacrifice. Fruit comes from sacrifice. The priestly way of life, which consists primarily of sacrifices, is a royal way of life, as it is

written: 'You are . . . a royal priesthood' (1 Peter 2:9).
The greatest deed of our Lord Jesus can be summed
up in a word: sacrifice. For us, too, the greatest, most
important and significant thing we can do is to offer
living sacrifices with prayer and fasting. That will
yield the greatest fruit and bring help even at this late
stage.

Thus we can understand why the Lord lamented
long ago through His prophet, 'I sought for a man
among them who should build up the wall and stand
in the breach before me for the land, that I should not
destroy it; but I found none' (Ezekiel 22:30). What a
heart-rending lament of God! He found no one who
could hold back the impending disaster, because no
one had offered himself as a living sacrifice. When in
time of war the enemy made a breach in the protec-
tive city wall, then only those who were prepared to
risk their lives and stand in the breach could hold
back the invading troops. Similarly, when a tidal
wave caused a breach in a dyke and the land was
about to be flooded, only men with a self-sacrificing
spirit dared form a human wall and step into the
breach so as to hold back the gushing waters. God is
now waiting for us to do the same in a spiritual sense.

The apostle Paul was a living testimony of this
priestly sacrifice. In him we see the dedication and
suffering involved in wrestling for the salvation of
souls: 'If my lifeblood is, so to speak, to be poured out
over your faith which I am offering up to God as a
sacrifice — that is, if I am to die for you — even then
I will be glad, and will share my joy with each of you'
(Philippians 2:17 LB) — 'I will most gladly spend and
be spent for your souls' (2 Corinthians 12:15; see also

2 Timothy 2:10; 4:6). Throughout Church history God has found martyrs. Whether martyrs of the body or of the soul, they offered themselves ardently. Love for the Lord Jesus was their motivation, not asceticism. Even though we may not yet be required to lay down our lives, God does wait for our response to His call, *I sought . . .* He longs for us to offer ourselves as a sacrifice, inspired by a fervent love for Him and our fellow beings, especially those of our own nation. God's heart must be aching as He looks upon this sin-laden world, which has added to its sins by blaspheming and mocking Jesus flagrantly. Unless there is repentance, judgment is inevitable. Should this not constrain us to offer priestly sacrifices out of thanksgiving for Jesus' sacrifice at Calvary, which is held in contempt by so many today?

With the sword of God's judgment poised over our nation — and many others — countless numbers threatened by eternal doom are waiting for our sacrifices. Everyone can offer 'living sacrifices', for these begin with small acts of denial. Everyone can do without some emotional, intellectual or material pleasure — for instance, the demand for love and attention, the desire for prestige. With destruction on our heels, do we not have the longing to 'fast' in some way to show that we are serious when we pray? How we would reproach ourselves later if we had not done everything we could to hold back divine judgment, seeing that God had given us the chance of doing so. By virtue of the all-sufficient sacrifice of Jesus we could have offered spiritual sacrifices. These are pure sacrifices with no ulterior motives such as pride, selfish ambition, self-will, envy. They do not inflate our ego and make us look down on others. Rather they spring from a penitent heart convicted by the holiness of God, accepting the truth about oneself and willing to take correction from others. If we pray with this attitude, our priestly supplications and intercession will be endowed with spiritual power.

In Britain, the United States and a number of other countries there are large groups who in these dark and perilous times intercede for their nations. As well as praying in their homes, they meet regularly for prayer gatherings often lasting the whole day or night. And these prayers are offered to the Lord with the sacrifice of food and sleep, for instance. At this crucial stage in world history the Lord expects us to be priestly intercessors, who underline their prayers with sacrifices and acts of denial. He is waiting for this more than ever before. Daniel, as we have already seen, responded to God's plea and lament, *I sought for a man among them who should build up the wall and stand in the breach before Me . . .* Daniel was a priestly soul and did not shrink back at the cost. Here was a man of whom the Lord could say, *I did find someone . . .* May God not have to lament over us as He did once through His prophet Ezekiel: *But I found none.*

So let us hear the Lord's summons today: *More sacrificial souls are needed.* Such souls would help to save our country, even though it is ripe for judgment, and God would be able to hear our prayers, just as He did in Daniel's case. What a responsibility has been placed on our shoulders at a time like this! We can make a difference and tip the balance. We have been given the opportunity of holding back God's arm, which is stretched out in judgment. But there is a condition: We need to pray with the right attitude, that is, with a humble, penitent, priestly and self-sacrificing spirit.

Knowing the Heart of God and Trusting Him

> *Prayer means lovingly bringing all the needs of our family, friends, neighbours and our nation, indeed, the whole world, before the Father and persisting in faith until help and salvation come.*

By praying with a priestly attitude and humbling himself beneath his sins, Daniel arrives at a moving conclusion: God's mercy is even greater than His righteousness. Thus Daniel can pray, 'To the Lord our God belong mercy and forgiveness' (v. 9). What a consolation!

To be sure, in his prayer Daniel repeatedly humbles himself before the holy God:

> The Lord our God is righteous in all the works which He does, though we have not obeyed His voice . . . We have sinned, we have done wickedly (Daniel 9:14-15 RAV).

It would seem that further calamities are inevitable. But Daniel is not filled with resignation. He knows what the heart of God is like. He has a personal relationship with Him. He knows that God is love and that He suffers immeasurably when people, especially those who call themselves believers, no longer take the commandments of God seriously or consider them binding for their lives; when they even sever themselves from God and reject Him, deliberately choosing sin and thus Satan. Daniel knows that such paths lead to ruin and how that grieves God, who in His love wants us to be happy.

This is why in his prayer Daniel refers three times to what God must suffer: 'the unfaithfulness which they have committed against *You*'; 'we have sinned against *You*'; 'we have sinned against *Him*' (Daniel 9:7,8,11 RAV, italics added). But how much greater God's heartache must be today when He looks upon our country and many other countries! Although Jesus laid down His life on the cross of Calvary as a sacrificial lamb for our salvation, man holds God and His commandments in contempt and the nations are coming increasingly under the control of sin.

A penitent sinner, however, rushes to his heavenly Father like the prodigal son, knowing that the Father's heart is full of mercy.

Because Daniel sees himself as a weak and sinful being, his prayer climaxes in the joy of finding refuge in the merciful heart of the Father. Against the backdrop of sin, apostasy, disobedience, and of God's righteousness, which really obliges Him to send judgment, it is as if the sun of grace suddenly comes out again. Now the forgiveness and abundant mercy of the Father shine forth, making Daniel bold and giving him the confidence that God's mercy will triumph over judgment. And so he calls upon the Lord, saying, 'To the Lord our God belong mercy and forgiveness.' This assurance strengthens Daniel's faith and helps him to reckon firmly with God's help in the time of great affliction. Yes, we call down God's help by trusting in His mercy.

Can the Father Help Us Today?

Priestly prayer means building a bridge for my neighbour, so that he may come home to the Father.

How many of us have a true concept of God our Father, from whom all fatherhood in heaven and on earth derives its name (Ephesians 3:15)? The heart of God rejoices when we turn to Him and grieves when we do not. It is hard for Him to punish us. When we have to suffer the consequences of our sinning, He is so full of pity that He speaks gently to us as He did to His people Israel while disciplining them: 'Is Ephraim my dear son? Is he my darling child? For as often as I speak against him, I do remember him still. Therefore my heart yearns for him; I will surely have mercy on him' (Jeremiah 31:20). When we are in distress, God cannot but help us, for His heart overflows with love and mercy.

However, there is a hindrance that keeps us from experiencing God's help. This is rebellion against His will and inward resistance to suffering, to the preliminary judgments of God in the form of natural disasters as well as to the scourge of terrorism, war and rioting. When we rebel instead of humbling ourselves like Daniel and admitting that we are receiving what our actions deserve, we prevent God from coming to our aid. We keep Him from fulfilling the promise He has so wonderfully fulfilled for others: 'I will rejoice in doing them good' (Jeremiah 32:41). God can manifest His goodness only when He finds the right conditions in us: a humble, trusting heart that believes in His fatherly love.

In this attitude of contrition Daniel is able to trust in God's mercy and to pray that unique prayer which countless numbers have prayed since then in times of affliction. As we now pray, let us do so with a humble, trusting heart and a priestly, sacrificial spirit:

> O my God, incline Your ear and hear;
> open Your eyes and see our desolations,
> and our land which as a Christian country
> is called by Your name;
> for we do not present
> our supplications before You
> because of our righteous deeds,
> but because of Your great mercies.
> (based on Daniel 9:18 RAV)

In answer to his prayer Daniel received the reply, 'you are greatly beloved' (v. 23), and the confirmation that his prayer was heard. God, who also loves us and our nations and suffers immeasurably because of our sins, does not desire our ruin. He desires our deliverance. However, He can grant deliverance only if He finds souls who will stand in the breach. Let us turn to Him in prayer like Daniel 'with fasting, sackcloth, and ashes', for we have a God who answers prayer.

Daniel's Prayer for Our Times

I set my face towards the Lord God
to make request
by prayer and supplications,
with fasting, sackcloth, and ashes.

O Lord, great and awesome God,
who keeps His covenant and mercy
with those who love Him,
and with those who keep
His commandments,
we have sinned and committed iniquity,
we have done wickedly and rebelled,
departing from Your precepts
and Your judgments.

Neither have we heeded
Your servants the prophets,
who spoke in Your name
to our people.

O Lord, righteousness belongs to You,
but to us shame of face,
as it is this day,
because of the unfaithfulness
which we have committed against You.

O Lord, to us belongs shame of face,
because we have sinned against You.

But to You, O Lord our God,
belong mercy and forgiveness,
though we have rebelled against You.

We have not obeyed
the voice of the Lord our God,
to walk in His laws,
which He set before us by His servants
the prophets. Yes, our people have
transgressed Your law, and have departed
so as not to obey Your voice;
therefore the curse
has been poured out on us,
because we have sinned against You.

And the Lord has confirmed His words,
which He spoke against us.

Yet we have not made our prayer
before the Lord our God,
that we might turn from our iniquities
and understand Your truth.

Therefore the Lord has kept
the disaster in mind,
and brought it upon us;
for the Lord our God is righteous
in all the works which He does,
though we have not obeyed His voice.

We have sinned,
we have done wickedly!

O Lord,
according to all Your righteousness,
let Your anger and Your fury
be turned away from our people.

Hear our prayers and supplications,
and for Your own sake
cause Your face to shine
on Your sanctuary, which is desolate.

O my God, incline Your ear and hear;
open Your eyes and see our desolations,
and our country
which as a Christian country
is called by Your name;
for we do not present
our supplications before You
because of our righteous deeds,
but because of Your great mercies.

O Lord, hear!
O Lord, forgive!
O Lord, listen and act!
Do not delay
for Your own sake,
my God.

(based on Daniel 9:3-19 RAV)

Prayer for Repentance

Dear Lord Jesus,

I ask You for what I long to have in my life: Your great gift of repentance. Send me by Your grace the Spirit of truth, that I may see myself in Your light and recognize the depths of my sin. Let Your Word convict me as Your standard for my thoughts and words, for what I do and fail to do, for my work and activities. Keep me from applying my own cheap standards. Let me take as binding the Ten Commandments and the standard of the Sermon on the Mount. Through them help me to see myself as You see me and to judge myself as You will judge me one day if I do not repent of my sin.

Through Your Holy Spirit help me to discern Your loving admonition in everything that happens to me, especially in Your chastening. And grant me the grace to respond to it willingly.

Hear my prayer and grant me a broken and contrite heart, not persisting in self-righteousness and self-complacency, but weeping over my sins and then rejoicing over Your forgiveness.

I thank You for the assurance that You will answer this prayer for daily contrition and repentance, because there is nothing that brings more joy to You than a sinner who repents and nothing You desire more from us than tears of repentance. So I will not look at my hard, impenitent heart. Rather, I will look to You, my Lord Jesus Christ. You came to destroy all self-righteousness and hardness of heart, and by Your redemption You have won for me a new heart, which is soft and humble.

Therefore, help me to persevere in prayer and faith until my hard heart has melted and I am able to weep over what I have done to God and to others. I know You will give me the grace to weep over my old, sinful nature, my harshness, lack of mercy and kindness, my gossiping, jealousy and envy, untruthfulness, false attachment to people and to the things of this world. You will bring about a complete change in me.

I thank You, O Lord, for You will create in me what I am lacking — repentance — so that my life will be completely transformed and that out of contrition divine life and love for You will grow in my heart. Through my life as a pardoned sinner, let me praise You here on earth and be prepared to celebrate with You the Marriage Feast of the Lamb in the heavenly glory.

Amen.

Watchmen for the Nation

Prayer means being called to be watchmen on His fortresses, not resting day or night until salvation, help and healing come to people's souls.

Prayer, which is the purpose and commission of our lives, does not only bring comfort and help for ourselves. There is far more to it. When we follow Jesus' challenge to pray, new vistas will suddenly open up and many changes will occur. Previously, we may have been resigned to the state of affairs and assumed an apathetic attitude: *What is the point in exerting ourselves if nothing can be altered?* But the Lord has given us the weapon of prayer. Now we have the opportunity to restrain the powers of darkness, save souls, experience divine intervention and mitigate the judgments of God.

For this reason I felt it was almost impossible to hear the daily news without giving an immediate response of prayer. In our sisterhood, whenever we hear of a new calamity or an act of violence or blasphemy, we say together, 'Lord, have mercy! Christ, have mercy! Lord, forgive us our sins!' It is because of our sins as individuals and as nations that God has to judge the world. As members of our nations, we share accountability for their sins, crimes and blasphemies.

Or when we hear reports of lawlessness, for instance, the killing of unborn human life, sexual perversion, drug addiction, and revolts, we pray together, 'Save souls, Lord! Save souls! Check the advance of the powers of darkness!'

When we see signs of our world being demonized and destroyed, we pray, 'Lord Jesus, You are the final Victor! You will make all things new!'

We can no longer go through life without giving the response of prayer. God is waiting for our prayers, since He longs to help, to change, to intervene and save. Fervent prayer for more souls to be saved — for Jesus' sake, and for the sake of His sacrifice and His outpoured blood — will reach the Father's heart.

Then lost souls will be saved. Captives of Satan will be freed. Those who have grown hard and indifferent will come to repentance. There will be signs of new life. The powers of darkness and destruction will be restrained. Terrorist attacks will be prevented. Screen and stage productions of blasphemous content will not be the success they were expected to be. Time and again we have seen this happen.

Through prayer we can still build a dam against the advancing powers of darkness. If only every town had a group of prayer warriors rising as one man to stem the tide of filth and demonism with the victorious name of Jesus! There is real power in calling upon the name of Jesus and in praising His blood. If we proclaim in faith ever anew 'Jesus is Victor!', then one day Satan has to yield. But if we do not call upon Jesus, we are giving the devil free rein. When Satan gains ground, countless numbers of people are led astray and fall into his clutches. By not praying, we fail others. Those who have a superficial, apathetic attitude towards life nowadays are not only lost themselves, but also to blame when others share the same fate.

Yet if we were to give ourselves to prayer now when sin and Satan are on the advance, we would find that we can still move God's arm as prayer warriors. Let us not say that we are too insignificant, incapable of assuming such responsibility, or argue that we ourselves are not much better. God's promises are especially meant for the humble and contrite of heart. The prayer of the humble pierces the clouds and reaches the heart of God. Nor let us say we have no time. How many minutes and hours make up a single day? How many opportunities would there be, if we were to take advantage of every minute? If we also use our work time when it does not require special concentration, we will find countless chances to send up short prayers over and again: 'Save souls, Lord. Save souls.'

At the judgment seat of Christ we will be asked whether we were in a state of constant prayer throughout the day, regardless of where we were or what we were doing. No one will be able to excuse himself then by saying that he had no time, for love drives us to pray for those who are enslaved by Satan, and heading for death and hell in eternity.

Widespread persecution of Christians and a major world disaster are impending. At a time like this we must help save those who are willing to be saved, by devoting ourselves to prayer and personal witnessing. That is our supreme commission and most urgent task in this day and age. What a tremendous privilege and blessing to be enrolled in the Lord's service, to share His concerns, to help Him save and rescue souls!

We Have a Glorious Hope

Prayer means crying out triumphantly in the darkness, 'Yes, Amen! It is finished! The almighty God has established His kingdom and Christ now reigns!'

German melody: Wir haben einen Felsen

We have a glo-rious hope____,

a hope that can-not die:

A - midst de-feat Christ's king-dom

in tri-umph will a - rise.

Lord, You are Life e - ter-nal,

and that life can-not end.

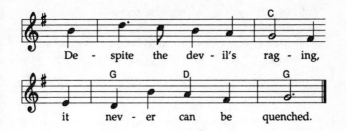

De - spite the dev - il's rag - ing,
it nev - er can be quenched.

2. We have a mighty Victor! Though Satan seems to
     win,
   Already he's defeated, for Jesus conquered him.
   Though darkness reigns, this hope makes our
     hearts rejoice and sing:
   Christ is the final Victor, from death His realm
     will spring.

3. For after persecution and judgment, there will be
   A mighty move of God and a great awakening.
   On earth will be a foretaste of heaven's realm of
     light,
   Where Father, Son and Spirit are ever glorified.

4. Rejoice, God's holy remnant will help to bring
     about
   A foretaste of the Saviour's eternal reign of love.
   So live in this assurance: His kingdom will arise,
   Defying death and Satan and all his evil lies.

5. Exalt the Lord triumphant, His majesty acclaim.
   With Him, destruction, suffering, have not the
     final say.

When hardships and repentance and tears have
paved the way,
He will renew the world and begin His glorious
reign.

Come, Let Us Raise a Victory Song

*May we shout for joy over your victory, and in the
name of our God set up our banners (Psalm 20:5).*

German melody: Triumphierend brach das Lamm

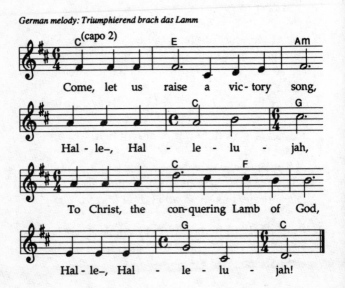

Come, let us raise a vic - tory song,

Hal - le—, Hal - le - lu - jah,

To Christ, the con - quering Lamb of God,

Hal - le—, Hal - le - lu - jah!

2. The devil's power is destroyed
   By Christ, the Lamb of God,
   And all the demons hell deployed
   Shall flee the precious blood.

3. The devil here has no more claim,
   Halle-, Hallelujah!
   Since Christ has plundered hell's domain,
   Halle-, Hallelujah!

4. When in this country havoc's planned,
   We will unite to pray,
   Until we move the Father's hand
   To intervene again.

5. May what the terrorists devised,
   Inspired by hell itself,
   Be overthrown, exposed in time,
   In answer to our cry.

6. The men of violence may wield
   Extensive power and might,
   But even greater is our faith
   In Christ, who won the fight.

7. From heaven You will intervene,
   Lord Jesus, without fail,
   Frustrating every wicked scheme
   While in its planning stage.

8. Angelic covering we claim
   For places under threat,

And none can penetrate this shield
Of angels standing guard.

9. Within our nation raise up souls
   To stem the tide of sin
   And to reclaim the land for God.
   The devil shall not win.

10. A praying people let us be
    Within the sanctuary,
    Pleading and standing in the breach,
    Claiming the victory.

11. From civil war deliver us,
    Terror and anarchy.
    Oh, save our land from perishing!
    Yours is the victory.

12. The victory cry reverberates:
    The battle is the Lord's.
    As vanguard Jesus leads the way,
    Subduing Satan's hordes.

13. So in the name of Jesus Christ
    Let us take up the fight,
    Assured the Lamb will always win,
    Putting the foe to flight.

14. The devil's cohorts are deposed,
    Disarmed and powerless.
    Their evil strategies are doomed:
    They will have no success.

15. We're not alone, for heaven's hosts,
    Alert and mobilized,
    Ready to help upon our plea,
    Are always at our side.

All Power Belongs to Christ Alone

The weapons of our warfare are not worldly but have divine power to destroy strongholds (2 Corinthians 10:4).

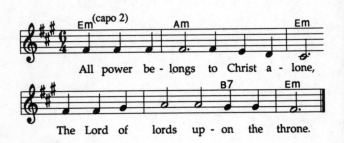

All power be-longs to Christ a-lone,
The Lord of lords up-on the throne.

2. Forevermore alive, He reigns
   And o'er the evil one prevails.

3. Our Saviour, risen from the grave,
   Subdues the demons in their rage.

4. The prince of darkness has to yield
   And bow to Christ, who reigns supreme.

5. Satanic strongholds fall this day.
   The wicked one has lost his sway.

6. Demonic forces flee from . . . (person/place)
   Exalted be the Lamb of God.

7. In . . . (place) Satan's overthrown.
    At Christ's command he has to go.

8. The devil has no power or hold,
    For Jesus died to save . . .'s soul.

9. Deception's power to entice
    Has been destroyed by Christ the Light.

10. Satan, begone: you're overthrown.
    Christ will establish here His throne.

Oh, Return, My Children

O my rebellious children, come back to me again and I will heal you from your sins. And they reply, Yes, we will come, for you are the Lord our God (Jeremiah 3:22 LB).

'Oh, re-turn, My chil-dren, oh, re-turn.'
Turn back to your lov-ing Fa-ther-God.
Won't you come?

2. Oh, return, drug addicts (etc.), oh, return,
   Turn back to your loving Father-God.
   Won't you come?

3. Oh, repent . . . , oh, repent.
   Turn back to your loving Father-God.
   Won't you come?

4. Hear Him calling, children; hear Him plead
   As He reaches out to you in love.
   Won't you come?

5. Turn away from sin, oh, turn away,
   That by Jesus Christ you may be saved.
   Won't you come?

6. Oh, be filled with sorrow for your sin,
   And you'll taste the Father's tender love.
   Won't you come?

7. Give your hearts to Jesus, give your hearts
   To the One who died to save us all.
   Won't you come?

8. See Him wait, O children, see Him wait.
   Will you not return to Him this day?
   Won't you come?

Awaken Souls

I have many people in this city (Acts 18:10).

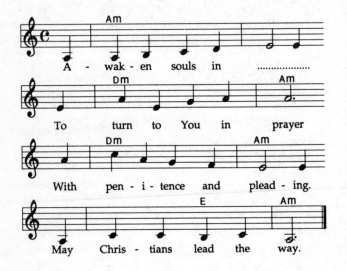

A - wak - en souls in ....
To turn to You in prayer
With pen - i - tence and plead - ing.
May Chris - tians lead the way.

Prayer of Repentance and Intercession for the Nation

Leader: O Lord, we bring our requests to You not on the basis of our righteousness, but on the basis of Your great mercy.

We confess with our nation:

All: *We have sinned. We have dared to turn away from Your holy and irrevocable commandments, which You gave to us as an expression of Your will. We have declared them irrelevant, invalid and no longer binding, even within the realm of the Christian Church. In so doing, we have opened the floodgates of sin.*

Leader: Father, in great distress we plead with You for our country, which deserves Your judgment.

All: *For the sake of Jesus' precious blood, have mercy upon our nation. Save our country from perishing. Accept our supplications, as we turn aside from paths of sin.*

Leader: We confess that as individuals and as a nation, we have sinned in an unprecedented way, allowing ourselves liberties contrary to Your commandments. This has resulted in immorality, licentiousness, drug addiction, alcoholism and perversions more vile than those of Sodom and Gomorrah.

All: *Each one of us who failed to make a stand against these sins is also to blame.*

Leader: Father, in great distress we plead with You for our country, which deserves Your judgment.

All: *For the sake of Jesus' precious blood, have mercy upon our nation. Save our country from perishing. Accept our supplications, as we turn aside from paths of sin.*

Leader: We confess that as individuals and as a nation, we have sinned, since the commandment, 'You shall not murder' has been widely violated. As a result, our country is flooded with terror, violence and unrest.

         Our nation is guilty of mass murder. The blood of millions of defenceless unborn children cries out to heaven.

         Unless we repent, Your sword of judgment will descend without fail. Death will come upon our land, perhaps in the form of a nuclear war, which will claim millions of lives.

         Your Word warns us that if we do not obey Your voice and keep Your commandments, death and calamity will overtake us.

All: *For the sake of Jesus' precious blood, have mercy upon our nation. Save our country from perishing.*

Accept our supplications, as we turn aside from paths of sin.

Leader: We confess with our nation that the most serious offence of all is being committed in our land — blasphemy against the living God. Never before has this sin been so public and widespread. It will bring a major judgment upon our country.

In deep grief we humble ourselves and lament that man dares to attack You, Almighty God, mocking and degrading You in an outrageous manner, blaspheming You in literature and in screen and stage productions.

All: *We confess that as Christians we, too, are guilty in as much as we have not made a stand against blasphemy and failed to give You the glory that is Your due as the holy triune God.*

Leader: Father, in great distress we plead with You for our country, which deserves Your judgment.

All: *For the sake of Jesus' precious blood, have mercy upon our nation. Save our country from perishing. Accept our supplications, as we turn aside from paths of sin.*

Leader: We confess that as individuals and as a nation, we are to blame that Satanism is able to spread so extensively in our country.

We confess with shame that even many who call themselves Christians are involved in occult practices. We come before You, Lord, in deep grief over the innumerable rock concerts and festivals subjecting thousands of young people to a demonic, spell-binding influence with fearful consequences.

All: *And so we cry to You to stop these satanic activities and to take away the satanic power and influence of such rock concerts.*

Leader: Father, in great distress we plead with You for our country, which deserves Your judgment.

All: *For the sake of Jesus' precious blood, have mercy upon our nation. Save our country from perishing. Accept our supplications, as we turn aside from paths of sin.*

Leader: O Lord, our God, hear our entreaties and accept our prayers in Your infinite mercy, for the sake of Your Son, who died an agonizing death on the cross for our sins.

We and our nation are provoking Your wrath. We are forcing You to send judgment because of the abominations mounting up to heaven. Yet we pray,

All: *Lord, forgive us our transgressions and be gracious unto us sinners. Help us to remain steadfast*

in prayer and supplication, and help us to turn from our sins with all our hearts.

Deliver our nation; defer the impending judgment, so that many souls may still be saved and those who love You may be prepared for the time of testing. Have mercy upon us for the sake of Jesus' precious blood.

Amen.

Prayer for Israel

May the blood of the Lamb cover Israel.

May the loving, suffering heart of the Father
draw His people to Himself.

May the creative power of the Holy Spirit
awaken contrition and repentance in them.

May our sorrow as Christians
seeking to make amends for the past
melt their hearts.

May the tears of the triune God
open their eyes to see the Redeemer.

Yes, the day is coming when they will behold
the One whom they have pierced
and weep for Him as for a first-born son.

For this we pray, knowing that God's gifts
and His call are irrevocable:
He will never go back
on His promises to His chosen people.

Amen.

Prayer in Times of Natural Disaster

Loving Father,
in these catastrophic weather conditions we come to
You. We thank You for the assurance that it is Your
loving, fatherly hand which is chastening us for our
good as individuals and as a nation.

We thank You
for the assurance that when You have attained the
goal Your loving will has set for us — that is, when
we turn from our sinful ways and come back to You
— You will show us grace again.

Our Father,
we humble ourselves before You and accept Your
judgment, for we are receiving what our actions
deserve. We and our nation have brought this judgment upon ourselves by our sins, which are mounting
up to heaven, and by offending Your divine holiness
with blasphemies such as the world has never seen.

Our Father,
for the sake of Jesus' outpoured blood, grant by Your
Holy Spirit that we and many in our nation will wake
up under this judgment.

We pray
that those who have turned away from You will start
praying again. May they cry to You in this distress
and give thanks for every gift they have received
from You.

We pray
that as a result of this judgment many who had been following paths of sin will accept Jesus' offer of salvation and begin a new life.

We pray
that You will renew in us the spirit of repentance, so that You can turn Your judgment into grace again and end the plight.

We pray,
help us to recognize this chastening as a preliminary judgment and help us to take it as an opportunity to practise for the coming times of testing by humbling ourselves deeply beneath Your chastening hand and submitting our wills wholly to Yours. Make us so one with You that we will be strong and not lose confidence in Your love when You are compelled to send even greater calamities in response to the sins of mankind.

Our Father,
for the sake of Jesus' outpoured blood, have mercy upon us in this severe plight and hear our prayer for help.

Amen.

Prayer in These Days of Terrorism

O Lord, our God, in great distress we call upon You, for You alone are our refuge and help.

We and our nation have sinned. We have been self-indulgent, seeking material wealth above all else. We have flouted Your commandments and even opened the doors to blasphemy. Now You have answered with the scourge of terrorism, which is threatening to ruin this and other countries. We call upon You in this time of fear and peril. Save us from our enemies. Let our supplications come before You. Mercifully hear our prayers for the sake of Jesus' outpoured blood.

We entreat You to prevent the terrorists from coming into power in our country.

Lord, have mercy, for You alone are our Helper, to whom all power is given in heaven and on earth.

Lord Jesus Christ, our mighty Victor, we plead with You to destroy their plans according to the scripture, 'Take counsel together, but it will come to nought.' Frustrate the plans of the terrorists.

Lord, have mercy, for You alone are our Helper, to whom all power is given in heaven and on earth.

We pray that further attempts at hostage-taking and assassination will not succeed. Cover potential targets with Your blood and protect them from all attacks.

Lord, have mercy, for You alone are our Helper, to whom all power is given in heaven and on earth.

Frustrate the schemes of the terrorists by creating disunity and confusion among them.

Lord, have mercy, for You alone are our Helper, to whom all power is given in heaven and on earth.

Graciously avert further assaults. Let bombs and other explosives be discovered in time and safely defused.

Lord, have mercy, for You alone are our Helper, to whom all power is given in heaven and on earth.

Prevent the theft of weapons, bank robberies, extortion and anything else that would assist or finance acts of violence planned by terrorists.

Lord, have mercy, for You alone are our Helper, to whom all power is given in heaven and on earth.

Prevent the infiltration of key positions by informers. May attempts to hinder the terrorists not fail owing to corruption.

Lord, have mercy, for You alone are our Helper, to whom all power is given in heaven and on earth.

Protect all those involved in the search for terrorists. Guide them in their decisions.

Lord, have mercy, for You alone are our Helper, to whom all power is given in heaven and on earth.

Help judges and all those appointed to uphold justice, so that in spite of their personal danger they will be true to the fundamental principles of law and justice.

Lord, have mercy, for You alone are our Helper, to whom all power is given in heaven and on earth.

May at least some of Your enemies, Lord Jesus, be delivered from the power of Satan. We pray that You would turn many a 'Saul' into a 'Paul'.

Lord, have mercy, for You alone are our Helper, to whom all power is given in heaven and on earth.

We pray that these critical times will serve to bring about a wholesome shock among Christians and in our nation, rousing us from all apathy and false security. Convict us ever anew of our sin, especially our rebelliousness, defiance, bitterness and hatred, by which we have contributed towards the advance of terrorism. Make us truly repentant, so that our prayers will come from the depths of a humbled heart and be effective.

Grant that Christians everywhere will be moved to pray and that many prayer groups will be formed, so that You can send help and prevent anarchy in this country.

Lord, have mercy, for You alone are our Helper, to whom all power is given in heaven and on earth.

Amen.

Prayer Against Blasphemy

Lord God,
You are the Creator of heaven and earth
and all mankind.
You are the eternal and immortal God.
And yet today You are blasphemed,
rejected and declared dead by man, whom You
    made.
Your commandments are held in contempt
even by Christians
and lie there trampled underfoot.

What have we done!
How could we dare to attack
the living God, who is our Judge!

Forgive us our sin.
Lord Jesus Christ, have mercy upon us
for the sake of Your precious blood.

Lord Jesus Christ,
You are the Son of God,
high and exalted,
of great majesty.
You are our Lord and Redeemer,
seated at the right hand of God.
Yet today, in innumerable
publications and performances,
You are blasphemed, degraded
and reduced to the image of a fool —
even within the Christian Church.

How grievously we have sinned against You
as a nation and as the Church!
You died for our sins
and we have responded with
mockery and blasphemy,
crowning You anew with thorns.

Forgive us our sin.
Lord Jesus Christ, have mercy upon us
for the sake of Your precious blood.

We who acknowledge You
as our Saviour and Redeemer
humble ourselves in shame
because of our own sins
and the sins of the Church and our nation.
Forgive us for not taking
our transgressions seriously.
Forgive us, Lord Jesus,
for remaining apathetic and unfeeling
when You were ridiculed and degraded.

How we have sinned against You!
We have abandoned You
in Your sufferings today,
even adding to Your grief.
We failed to pray and plead
in view of our sins
as individuals and as a nation.
We did not repent of all the wrongdoing.
We even condoned it.

Forgive us our sin.

Lord Jesus Christ, have mercy upon us
for the sake of Your precious blood.

Let us rise from sleep
and begin to wrestle in prayer.

In view of all the blasphemies
prevalent in our times,
we want to bear witness to You,
Jesus our Redeemer,
and to You, the holy God and Judge.
We are prepared to pay the cost
in terms of sacrifice and suffering.

Holy Spirit, help us to do so.
Kindle our hearts to pray with ardour
in contrition and repentance.
Kindle us with the desire
to make sacrifices and bear suffering
for Jesus, our despised Lord.

Lord Jesus, we long to love You
in the measure that You are hated today.

Lord Jesus, we want to stand up
and be counted for You.
Help us to seize every opportunity
to speak out against blasphemy.
Help us to make a stand against
the defamation of Your character
in films and publications,
and especially within the Christian Church.

O Lamb of God,
by the power of Your blood
prevent the forces of evil
from advancing.
Save souls from lives of sin
and from blasphemy against God.

Through prayer and repentance
may we be prepared, so that when
Your great judgment passes over the earth,
You will be able to rescue us.

Amen.

* * *

My Jesus is weeping, lamenting today,
Derided, degraded, a figure of shame.
No heart ever loved us so tenderly,
Yet none is so wounded or caused such grief.

We yearn to uplift You as never before;
Oh, open our ears to perceive, dear Lord,
Your weeping, lamenting, Your heart's grief and
    pain,
That we may bring comfort to You today.

We yearn now to love You, live for You alone,
With all our hearts share in Your suffering
    and woe.
We want to proclaim all that You mean to us,
That many may know You, Lord Jesus Christ.

Prayer for Youth into Rock

Lord Jesus Christ,

Rescue souls before a major judgment
comes upon the world
because of the sins mounting up to heaven.

Lamb of God, Your blood flowed
for the salvation of all people.
You have power over Satan and his attacks.
Demonstrate Your victorious power
over the satanic rock concerts,
which are leading countless numbers into sin.

Bind Satan's power,
so that not so many young people
are carried away by this demonic frenzy.

Lord Jesus Christ,
have mercy and rescue
more and more of our youth
during this time of grace
before judgment descends.
You are the Saviour
and shed Your blood for them, too,
so that they need not suffer
the punishment of hell.
Grant that they will come to repentance
before it is too late.

You know that many of them
grew up hearing that rebellion,

lying, immorality and violence are the norm,
that God's commandments are no longer relevant,
that the main thing is the liberation of man,
liberation from every commandment and
     regulation —
and that this is what life is all about.
So we ask You to have mercy on them
and to forgive us where we, as the older
     generation,
have been a negative influence for them.

Hear our prayer and take away
from the rock stars their demonic power
as we proclaim the blood of the Lamb over them.
Take away their ability to fascinate,
so that they cannot bring
thousands of young people
under their satanic influence.

You can bring individual rock singers
to repentance, yes, to faith in You,
and make them witnesses of Your saving power.

You can alert young people
to the terrible end of many rock stars,
so that they stop idolizing them.
You can take away their pleasure and interest
in this satanic entertainment.

You are a God who hears prayer,
and so we believe that You will intervene
when we call to You.

                                        Amen.

Protection in a Satanic Age

Prayer means stepping into battle in the assurance that the greater the onslaught of Satan, the greater will be the victory God has for us.

We are living in a time of worldwide occultism. Occult practices such as seances, putting curses on others and the usage of dubious medication and charms are on the rise. The mass media are swamped with occult themes. It is made to appear sensational and fascinating to explore the supernatural realms, where there are so many new things to discover. Just as people have hobbies, many are turning with keen interest to the occult — usually without knowing or suspecting that by doing so they are coming under an extremely dangerous power that could ruin their lives now and for all eternity. Others who do not feel attracted to this occult fad regard it all as nonsense, and thus they, too, think it harmless. They feel sorry for Christians who take the matter seriously, who have a 'medieval faith' and believe that Satan and his underlings, witches and sorcerers, exist and are at work today.

Occultism, however, is not a harmless matter. People will not remain unscathed, even if they think that their interest is purely scientific. They cannot experiment with such things without attracting Satan and coming under his influence. He is alive and has been given power. And he makes use of this power to harm people, torment them and lead them into destruction.

In the Bible we read that all occult activities are an abomination to the Lord. 'There shall not be found among you anyone who makes his son or his daughter pass through the fire, or one who practises witchcraft, or a soothsayer, or one who interprets omens, or a sorcerer, or one who conjures spells, or a medium, or a spiritist, or one who calls up the dead. For all who do these things are an abomination to the Lord' (Deuteronomy 18:10-12 RAV).

Anyone who risks dabbling in the occult is exposing himself to danger. But what about those who are innocent and who have come under satanic curses without having had anything to do with the occult? It is a frightening thought that no one can know whether a curse is being put on him. If anyone hates us, feels that we are in his way or simply takes a dislike to us, without any provocation on our part, he can easily find someone to put a curse on us, so that a serious calamity would strike us, our family, home, business or anything else that belongs to us.

Yet even though this is true, let us remember that we have a sure refuge — our Lord Jesus Christ. Those who call upon Him will experience deliverance from such spells. Those who truly believe in Jesus Christ as their Saviour and have the right relationship with Him can cancel the effect of these curses by claiming the blood of Jesus Christ. The blood of Jesus is a shield against the evil one's attacks. Satan flees when he sees us beneath the cross of Jesus and covered by the blood of the Lamb. If we claim the blood of the Lamb, we will experience its invincible power.

Nowadays not only are people affected by curses and other practices of witchcraft, but buildings, fields, indeed, entire districts and cities are brought under the power of darkness. What an assurance it is for us in these times to know that we can pronounce the name of Him who is stronger than Satan and all his wiles, to whom Satan is subject and whom he must obey! It is the name of Jesus! Now we are called to follow the example of our forefathers, who used to pray for protection from the evil one's attacks.

> You hordes of hell, now take to flight!
> You have no right to harm us.
> This house in safety shall remain,
> For it belongs to Jesus.
> A mighty host of angel-guards
> Surround it like a wall,
> Watch over it and shelter it.
> Depart, you hordes of hell.
>
> Christian Scriver 1629-1693

For us, too, the time has come to take the powers of evil seriously and to claim protection from them. Today, as in no previous age, Satan is prowling around like a roaring lion, bent on causing havoc, tormenting people and destroying all the good things God has given them. However, the enemy must pay attention to prayers like the above that are raised to heaven day by day. Satan is forced to retreat when the name of Jesus is pronounced over houses, property, towns and people's souls. He must yield when they are placed under the sign of Jesus' cross, the sign of victory, and covered by His blood.

Today we can really appreciate the significance of Jesus shedding His blood for us at Calvary. Indeed, as seldom before, we can experience the power of Jesus, the Lamb of God, and the power of His blood. Today the time has come for us to worship the Lamb. This is the challenge of the Book of Revelation, the book for the end times. The more we worship the Lamb and praise His wounds and the power of His blood, the more we will experience His protection from all the attacks and deceptions of the evil one.

When we worship Jesus, we are honouring Him as the almighty Lord and Master, who commands the powers of darkness to flee. And He will demonstrate His power. Since Satan is a created being, a fallen angel, he must bow to the will of God. He trembles when the name of Jesus is pronounced. He yields when the power of Jesus' blood is claimed. Jesus said, 'I have given you authority . . . over all the power of the enemy; and nothing shall hurt you' (Luke 10:19).

Thus we need not be afraid and fall into despair, even though curses and spells are being pronounced today. Jesus Christ alone is omnipotent. All things are subject to Him.

Nevertheless, calling upon Jesus and praising His blood will be effective only if there is no unforgiven and uncleansed sin in our lives. Harbouring sin gives Satan a right to us. But if we walk in the light, that is, confess our sins and turn from them, we will receive forgiveness. Then when we call upon Jesus and claim His redeeming blood, our prayers will be heard.

Prayers for Protection Against Curses

> *They have conquered him [Satan] by the blood of the Lamb (Revelation 12:11).*

O Lamb of God, by Your shed blood,
And by Your name, O Jesus,
We claim protection for this place
From Satan's raging forces.
There's power in Christ Jesus' cross,
The cross of victory.
It overcomes the hordes of hell
And forces them to flee.

Amen.

* * *

O Jesus, may Your gracious hand
Protect and guard our home and land.
Your holy blood our refuge be
Against the raging enemy.
Your cross, the sign of victory,
Makes Satan's forces turn and flee.
And so, Lord Jesus, may Your cross
Be placed upon our land and house,
That by this sign they may be known
As being Yours, and Yours alone.
Protection for this place we claim,
Lord Jesus, in Your precious name.
It is the mightiest of powers,
And guards home, land, and souls of ours.

Amen.

The Victory's Won

Prayer means taking refuge in Jesus' wounds and finding healing there when I am painfully aware of my sins.

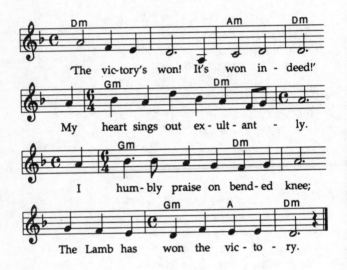

'The vic-tory's won! It's won in - deed!'
My heart sings out ex - ult - ant - ly.
I hum - bly praise on bend - ed knee;
The Lamb has won the vic - to - ry.

2. The victory stands; yes, I am free
   From all of Satan's tyranny.
   You cried, 'It's finished!' on the tree;
   You ransomed me at Calvary.

3. My fetters fall; the victory's won.
   The foe lies vanquished on the ground.
   Your holy blood has ransomed me,
   For Yours, Lord, is the victory.

4. In darkest night and misery
   I'll always see the victory.
   The devil lost his claim to me,
   For Jesus won the victory.

5. O Lamb, I praise You without end;
   Such love I'll never comprehend.
   'It's finished!' You cried on the tree,
   As You laid down Your life for me.

On Calvary You Won the Fight

Prayer means singing the joyful song of salvation over every sin, for the One to whom we pray has already broken the power of sin on the cross.

2. Now every demon must depart
   Through Jesus' power from . . .'s heart.

3. The vanquished foe now has to flee,
   For Christ has won the victory.

4. The blood of Christ brings . . . release
   From every demon's influence.

5. All power belongs to Jesus Christ;
   The devil's sceptre broken lies.

6. Now . . . belongs to Jesus Christ;
   For (him/her) He paid the ransom price.

7. The Lamb has won the victory,
   Destroying Satan's tyranny.

8. My Saviour lives, today He lives!
   In . . . 's life He victory gives.

9. The devil lost his claim on . . .
   When Jesus died at Calvary.

10. Christ lives, triumphant o'er His foes;
    The devil's hold He overthrows.

11. All hail the power of Jesus' wounds,
    The victory gaining for . . . 's soul.

12. Behold, our risen Lord will quell
    The wrath of Satan and of hell.

13. His sacrifice avails for . . . ,
    Redemption bringing, full release.

14. Christ Jesus won the victory,
    The devil's captive setting free.

15. We claim Your blood, Lord Jesus Christ,
    And You destroy the demons' might.

16. I trust the power of Your blood
    To heal, restore and overcome.

17. The precious blood of Christ we claim.
    The powers of darkness it restrains.

Demons Confounded and Terror-Stricken

Prayer means in faith to set foot in the enemy's territory and there to raise the sign of victory, which is the cross.

German melody: Gott ist die Liebe

De- mons con - found- ed and ter-ror - strick- en,

No more se - cure is their prince's throne.

It has be - gun to shake, re- minding of the day

When Je- sus comes a- gain as Lord and Judge.

repeat last line of music at the end of verse 4

2. Prayer missiles flying, victory securing,
   The demon prince is fast losing grip.
   He flails and flounders at each encounter,
   One final blow all his might destroys.

3. So keep on praying, the day is coming
   When he'll be routed once and for all.
   His throne is swaying, his power is waning,
   His evil empire condemned to fall.

4. In all creation there's jubilation
   For . . . is free from his tyranny.
   We'll see a moving, a fresh outpouring,
   Of God's own Spirit where Satan ruled.
   Praise to the Lamb for His victory!

Dethroned Will Be This Demon Prince

Prayer means ever looking to the cross of Jesus Christ, where the opposition of the enemy has already been overcome.

De - throned will be this de - mon prince,
Whose thirst for souls is nev - er stilled.
Lo, his throne is col - laps - ing!
A sin - gle word from Je - sus Christ
Strikes ter - ror in his e - vil mind
And caus - es him to trem - ble.

2. The saints are praying — well he knows! —
   His throne is shaking down below
   There in the hellish regions.
   He feels it shudder at each blow.
   The time has come for him to go,
   Vanquished by Christ the Victor.

3. Oh, let us raise the victory strain
   And pave the way for Jesus' reign
   Amid hell's howling protest.
   The demons sense the end is near,
   And soon their prince will disappear,
   Defeated and confounded.

4. Indeed, that moment's not far off.
   In faith we look unto the cross,
   Trusting in Jesus' victory.
   The power of His precious blood
   Will bring release to . . . ,
   The devil's hold destroying.

Praise Be to You,
O Holy Lamb of God

Prayer means claiming the blood of the Lamb as we come to the Father. Since Jesus was inflicted with wounds for the sake of our redemption, how can the Father refuse our pleas when we take refuge in the wounds of His only Son?

2. Praise be to You, O holy Lamb of God.
   You gave Your lifeblood to redeem us,
   Sinners in need of divine salvation
   Through Your blood's redemptive, atoning
      power.

3. Praise be to You, O holy Lamb of God.
   Your precious, saving blood You offer,
   For it has power unlimited
   To redeem and free us from sin and bondage.

4. Praise be to You, O holy Lamb of God.
   Your precious, saving blood contains
   Power to transform beyond all recognition,
   Making saints of sinners, once captives of Satan.

5. Praise be to You, O holy Lamb of God.
   From Your deep wounds there flows a river
   Of precious, healing and saving blood
   For all who kneel at the foot of the cross in
      contrition.

6. Praise be to You, O holy Lamb of God.
   With Your own lifeblood as an off'ring
   You have prepared the communion table
   And invite us to share in life divine.

7. Praise be to You, O holy Lamb of God.
   You did not come to save the righteous,
   But gave Your blood for the undeserving,
   Those who regard themselves as poor and
      wretched sinners.

8. Praise be to You, O holy Lamb of God.
   Your precious lifeblood pleads forgiveness
   For contrite, penitent souls, who grieved You
   And who truly seek to make amends.

9. Praise be to You, O holy Lamb of God.
   Your precious blood avails for sinners,
   Covering all evil thoughts and actions
   When we bring them to You and claim Your
       pardon.

10. Praise be to You, O holy Lamb of God.
    Your precious, saving blood has power
    To cleanse us from every sin committed,
    So that in Your sight we are whiter than snow.

11. Praise be to You, O holy Lamb of God.
    Curative, healing powers lie hidden
    Within Your saving and precious blood,
    Healing and relief to our sin-sick hearts bringing.

12. Praise be to You, O holy Lamb of God.
    Your outpoured blood is our robe of honour
    With which You'll clothe us when we are
        summoned
    Into the presence of God that we may stand
        before Him.

13. Praise be to You, O holy Lamb of God.
    Your lifeblood sets us free from all those
    Who seek to bind our souls to themselves.
    Your blood will sever and cancel all false
        attachments.

14. Praise be to You, O holy Lamb of God.
    Your sacred wounds are like a fountain
    Flowing so freely for man's redemption,
    Cleansing, healing all who would drink these
       waters.

15. Praise be to You, O holy Lamb of God.
    You bid us come to drink at all times
    From this fount filled with Your precious blood,
    For it will transform and completely renew us.

16. Praise be to You, O holy Lamb of God.
    Sick, weary bodies are refreshed
    Through Your life-giving, sustaining blood,
    If we trust and claim in faith its power.

17. Praise be to You, O holy Lamb of God.
    Your precious lifeblood unites us with You
    When we partake of this gift in faith,
    For we then abide in You, and You in us.

18. Praise be to You, O holy Lamb of God.
    When Your blood flowed down from the cross,
    You crushed the head of the evil serpent,
    Overthrowing Satan's kingdom of darkness.

19. Praise be to You, O holy Lamb of God.
    When Your own claim the blood in faith,
    All Satan's forces are put to flight,
    Driven away by its power to vanquish and
       conquer.

•

20. Praise be to You, O holy Lamb of God.
    Your outpoured blood has power to cancel
    Each curse and spell that is placed upon us
    By those inspired by the devil and his fallen
        angels.

21. Praise be to You, O holy Lamb of God.
    Your outpoured blood defeated Satan,
    Breaking this tyrant's authority
    And confounding every attack against us.

22. Praise be to You, O holy Lamb of God.
    Your outpoured blood spells victory for us
    Over the devil and all his legions,
    So that we can emerge from the war in triumph.

23. Praise be to You, O holy Lamb of God.
    Your sacred wounds are signs of victory
    Forcing the devil to yield in haste
    When in faith we praise and claim their power.

24. Praise be to You, O holy Lamb of God.
    Your outpoured blood has power and might
    To break apart every chain and fetter
    By which demons hold us in sinful bondage.

25. Praise be to You, O holy Lamb of God.
    Demon hosts flee and all hell trembles
    At the mere sound of our praise and worship
    Of the precious blood of the Lamb, who
        triumphed.

26. Praise be to You, O holy Lamb of God.
    Protecting power lies in Your blood,
    Safeguarding people and homes and lands
    From the wiles of the devil and all his
       onslaughts.

27. Praise be to You, O holy Lamb of God.
    What great power lies within Your blood,
    The power of never-ending life,
    Strengthening, healing, refreshing, restoring and
       blessing!

28. Praise be to You, O holy Lamb of God.
    Through Your blood, shed for our transgressions,
    We may partake of Your nature divine:
    Love, patience, meekness, humility, trust and
       dedication.

29. Praise be to You, O holy Lamb of God,
    Bearing scars shining like precious rubies,
    The price You paid for mankind's redemption!
    Angelic choirs pay tribute in ceaseless worship.

30. Praise be to You, O holy Lamb of God.
    You will fulfil what You have promised:
    'Behold and see, I make all things new!'
    Through Your outpoured blood You will bring
       renewal.

31. Praise be to You, O holy Lamb of God.
    One day all mankind will adore You
    For bringing forth by Your blood the new earth
    Out of the chaos and ruins of a dying creation.

Pronouncing Blessings

Prayer means pleading for the salvation of our dear ones and many others, by blessing them with the name of Jesus.

Praying for others includes blessing them. Holy Scripture says we are called to be a royal priesthood (1 Peter 2:9). Part of an Old Testament priest's vocation was to pronounce blessings on others, that is, to put the name of God upon people (Numbers 6:23-27). This is a way for us to pray for others, even during our daily activities. We can make use of every encounter with people to bless them with the name of Jesus. We should practise pronouncing blessings, for great power lies in this kind of prayer. There are so many opportunities to give to others. Each time we greet someone or shake hands, we can silently bless that person with the name of Jesus. Depending on his or her particular need, we can also add one of the Lord's attributes: Jesus your Victor, Helper, Comforter, Saviour. People are transformed when a blessing is invoked on them.

Litany of Blessing

May Jesus bless you by making His name shine upon you and dispelling all darkness.

May the Holy Spirit bless you with His truth, as He brings all hidden sin into the light of God.

May the Holy Spirit bless you with the grace of repentance, which will create new life in you.

May Jesus bless you with a victorious faith in Him, the risen Lord, beneath whose feet every power of sin and death is laid.

May the Lamb of God bless you with the power of His blood, which will protect you from every onslaught of the evil one.

May Jesus Christ bless you with the spirit of joy, so that you will shine forth His joy.

May the Lord bless you with His peace, so that your heart and mind are kept in Him and your will rests in His.

May Jesus bless you with the patience of the Lamb, so that you may quietly endure suffering, always showing patience to others.

May Jesus Christ bless you with His love, so that you can love with the love that bears all things, endures all things, hopes all things.

May the holy triune God, Father, Son and Holy Spirit, bless you so that you might live to His glory.

Amen.

Jesus, Radiant Morning Star

Prayer means lovingly repeating one name above every other name: JESUS.

2. Jesus, blessed be Your name,
    Saviour, Lord and Advocate.
    When we call to You in faith,
    You will hasten to our aid
    As the conquering Lord of lords,
    Who defeated Satan's hordes.

3. Jesus, in Your name resides
    Power from God and life divine,
    Quickening our slumb'ring souls,
    Healing, saving, making whole.
    Miracles occur today
    When we call upon Your name.

4. Jesus, name victorious,
    Wonderful and glorious,
    Bringing help and victory,
    Breaking Satan's tyranny,
    Granting blessings, grace divine,
    Healing damaged souls and minds.

5. Jesus, name of brilliant light
    Putting Satan's hordes to flight,
    Blessed be Your holy name
    With its strength and power to save,
    Mighty shield to ward off blows,
    Driving off the fiercest foes.

6. Jesus, name of saving grace,
    Of redemption fully paid,
    Cleansing all our sinful stains,
    Silencing the devil's claims,
    Name above all names on earth
    And throughout the universe.

7. Jesus, blessed, saving name
   Expiating guilt and shame,
   Rescuing from sinful bonds,
   Overcoming fears and qualms.
   Jesus, name of majesty,
   Heavenly authority.

8. Jesus, Jesus, is the cry
   Ringing through the earth and sky.
   Jesus, solace in distress,
   Sun of grace and righteousness,
   And by Your life-giving rays
   You alone the world sustain.

9. Jesus, Jesus, Prince of Peace,
   Mediator, Mercy-Seat,
   Jesus, Jesus, Lamb of God,
   Saving us upon the cross,
   Cancelling our guilt and debts,
   Bringing us the Father's grace.

10. Jesus! Jesus! angel choirs
    Praise this name with hearts afire.
    Jesus brings us peace of soul,
    Soothing us in all our woe.
    Jesus overthrew the foe,
    Jesus died to save us all.

11. Jesus, Jesus! is the cry
    Ringing through the earth and sky.
    Jesus, Jesus, You alone
    Shall receive acclaim, renown.
    Jesus, blessed Son of God,
    Be my one and only Lord.

12. Jesus! sing God's people here
    And throughout the heavenly sphere.
    Jesus! Majesty divine
    From whom heaven's splendour shines,
    Image of the Father-God,
    Source of comfort, joy untold.

13. Jesus! cries this captive earth
    In the grip of sin and death.
    Jesus! shouts the heavenly host.
    Jesus! shouts the earth below.
    Jesus! all of nature shouts,
    For it ever serves its God.

14. Jesus! stars and moon and sun
    Clouds and wind in unison
    Raising songs of joyful praise
    For the bounty of Your grace.
    Jesus! all the peoples sing,
    Jesus! ransoming from sin.

15. Jesus, mighty Champion,
    King of kings upon the throne.
    Jesus! land and water sing
    With all creatures, living things.
    Jesus! the world tribute pays
    To their Lord and Potentate.

Give God the Glory

Prayer means lovingly contemplating the Father, the Son and the Holy Spirit, allowing our hearts to be enkindled to praise and adore the love and omnipotence of the most blessed Trinity.

One prayer in particular should sound louder than all others in the present hour of darkness. It is a powerful prayer. It is the prayer of the first Christians at a time of great distress: a prayer that caused the place where they were gathered to shake. With this particular prayer the believers besieged heaven, gaining access to the throne of God — and His answer came mightily, as related in Acts 4. Simple though it was, this prayer must have pleased God greatly and been very effective. It was a prayer in adoration of the omnipotent Creator and immortal God.

Significantly enough, the Lord is calling us to such prayer in the end times. We have come full circle. At the beginning of the Christian era, the name of Jesus was blasphemed and the believers were widely persecuted. At the close of the age Jesus is blasphemed once again — not only in one country, but throughout the world, in every nation and even in the Christian Church. Believers are coming under growing pressure as satanic forces stir up hatred towards Jesus and His followers.

The primary prayer of the New Testament Church was not *Lord, protect us, help us.* In the face of distress and persecution a mighty anthem of adoration rose to God from the assembled believers: 'O Lord, Creator of heaven and earth and of the sea and everything in them' (Acts 4:24 LB). What power lies in this statement! It echoes the awe and wonder of praying men and women in the Old Testament and the cry of the Psalmist: *O Lord, who is like You? There is no God like You!* Continuing in this vein, the New Testament believers prayed, 'Why do the heathen rage against the Lord, and the foolish nations plan their little plots against Almighty God?' (v.25 LB). For these Christians it was an established truth: God is always greater, even when 'the kings of the earth unite to fight against him, and against the anointed Son of God' (v. 26 LB).

Should that not be our prayer today? In this day and age there is a universal revolt against God. Great effort is being made to discredit Jesus Christ and His followers and to do away with them.

Our Lord and Saviour, Jesus Christ, the innocent Lamb of God, who in His selfless and long-suffering love gave Himself for us, even sacrificing His life on the cross, and rose again in triumph, is made to wear the sin-stained garment of mankind today. Violence, rebellion, hatred, murder, terrorism — every imaginable crime is attributed to Him. The holy Son of God is publicly degraded through such malicious defamation of character, paraded, as in a triumphal procession, throughout the nations in films, television programmes and publications. Man dares to attack God Himself. Man not only abolishes God's commandments but blasphemes Him; and according to His Word, blasphemy is punishable with death (Leviticus 24:16).

The mighty summons by the angel in Revelation 14 was addressed to all the inhabitants of the earth, every nation, tribe and tongue. It is especially relevant today when the whole earth has become a family of nations, equally guilty of the blasphemies against Jesus. It comes like a last warning signal.

> Fear God and give him glory, for the hour of his judgment has come; and worship him who made heaven and earth, the sea and the fountains of water (Revelation 14:7).

At a time when society is becoming increasingly anti-authority and man is encouraged to take God's place, no appeal to prayer could be more appropriate than the clarion call, *Give God the glory!*

Glory be to God! Glory be to the Lamb! This is the prayer God is waiting for today, as He has revealed in His Word. If we were to unite in exalting God, what tremendous results there would be! Before the visible and invisible world the holy, immortal God and Creator, our Lord who is widely blasphemed today, would once more receive the honour that is His due as the Almighty. Blasphemy will be the main cause for the coming judgment. Glorification of God and the Lamb would therefore have a restraining effect. It would hold back Satan's final show of power and thus defer the ensuing devastation.

Such worship would have yet another effect. It would make us strong in the time of testing. This is

GIVE GOD THE GLORY 89

what happened to the first Christians, who in their peril went on to pray, 'Grant to your servants great boldness in their preaching' (Acts 4:29 LB). Although two of their number, Peter and John, had just been released from prison with the warning never again to speak about Jesus, and although their own lives were endangered, they prayed that God would enable them to testify publicly to Him all the more. By worshipping God and storming heaven with a bold faith, they received the strength to continue to bear witness to the name of Jesus under persecution.

Nearly twenty centuries later we, too, need the strength to face Christian persecution, and through praise and worship we will become strong. Let us therefore unite in prayer to exalt the name of Jesus, to acclaim His glorious victory at Calvary, and to worship the holy, eternal, immortal Creator God, our Father, for His love and omnipotence. Can we imagine the impact of such united prayer on a worldwide scale? Our worship would resound throughout the heavens and bring joy to the heart of God amid all the blasphemy. Moreover, it would have a counteractive effect. On earth it would still curb the advance of sin and Satan. It would form a stronghold against the waves of demonism from the abyss as they encroach upon the land, seeking to deluge everything.

The Holy Spirit quite naturally leads God's own from repentance, the humbling of self, and intercession on to adoration, since this is the Lord's summons for praying people in our times. Let us obey His command, for prayer offered according to His will (1 John 5:14) has a great promise attached. Let us give thanks to God for having given us in the darkness of our

times such a wonderful calling, which will also bring
us strength and joy in our personal lives — the calling
to give God the glory!

* * *

Who is like God?
There is no God like You,
Neither above in heaven
Nor here below on earth.

O Lord, we worship You,
Yours is the glory and majesty!
All the realms of heaven
Are filled with Your great glory,
Resplendent with Your radiance and light.

Mighty and great are Your deeds, O Lord.
Unsearchable are Your purposes,
O Sovereign Lord and King!
Wisely You govern all destiny!
From age to age You rule with power.
Firm stands Your throne
For ever and for evermore!

Notes

-25, Daniel: A Man of Prayer
... from *O Lord, hear!*, a newsletter first published in German in September 1983. First English edition in October 1983.

pp. 26-27, Prayer for Repentance
Taken from *Repentance – The Joy-Filled Life*, pp. 85-86, first published in German in 1959. First English edition in 1968.

pp. 28-31, Watchmen for the Nation
Taken from *Countdown to World Disaster – Hope and Protection for the Future*, pp. 71-75, first published in German in 1973. First English edition in 1974. Out of print.

pp. 43-47, Prayer of Repentance and Intercession for the Nation
Originally written for the International Day of Prayer and Repentance on August 17, 1974.

pp. 49-50, Prayer in Times of Natural Disaster
Simultaneously printed in German and English in summer 1976 during catastrophic weather conditions in Europe.

pp. 51-54, Prayer in These Days of Terrorism
Simultaneously printed in German and English in September 1977.

pp. 59-60, Prayer for Youth into Rock
Taken from *Rock Music – Where from, Where to?*, pp. 25-27,

first published in German in 1989. First English edition in 1990.

pp. 61-65, Protection in a Satanic Age
Taken from *Escaping the Web of Deception*, pp. 43-52, first published in German in 1975. First English edition in 1975.

pp. 86-90, Give God the Glory
Taken from the newsletter *A Continuation of the International Day of Prayer and Repentance on August 17, 1974*. Simultaneously printed in German and English in November 1974.

Supplementary Literature
by M. Basilea Schlink

NATURE OUT OF CONTROL? 96 pages

In view of the recent floods, fires, quakes and blizzards, people are beginning to ask, 'Is God trying to tell us something?'

YOURS IS THE VICTORY AND MAJESTY 96 pages

Readers comment: How wonderfully the Spirit explains everything to God's children! * The best analysis of the present situation I've come across. Profound, discerning.

STRONG IN THE TIME OF TESTING 96 pages

As Christians face growing pressures, the need to prepare for the testing of our faith is even more urgent than when these texts and prayers were originally written. As Mother Basilea encouragingly shares, in Jesus Christ we can find all the grace we need to stand the test of suffering.

DOES OUR WORLD HAVE A FUTURE? 48 pages

Directing our attention to the Bible, the author opens up for us an unusual perspective of the future.

ISRAEL, MY CHOSEN PEOPLE 128 pages

Identifying herself with the guilt of her nation in the Third Reich, Mother Basilea stresses the need of a nation-wide repentance, beginning with the Christians. Compassionately and with prophetic insight she traces God's dealings with His beloved people up to their return to the land of their fathers and focuses on the time when Israel will attain her glorious destiny to be a blessing for all nations.

MORE PRECIOUS THAN GOLD 192 pages

A word of comfort, a challenge or a promise for every day of the year. In God's rules for living lies the key to His blessing upon our family, community and nation.

I WILL GIVE YOU THE TREASURES OF DARKNESS 48 pages

'This booklet is an excellent spiritual counsellor in print. Whenever depression comes upon me, whenever I have to pass through a time of darkness, here I find where it all comes from and the purpose. There is so much depth to this interpretation. You can sense that it is real and based on personal experience.'

PRAYING OUR WAY THROUGH LIFE 48 pages

'. . . came just at the right moment in my life. I was asking questions of Him: "Why again?" This booklet answered my questions and I praised Him for His timing.'

MIRROR OF CONSCIENCE 32 pages

'I have just finished reading *Mirror of Conscience*, which has made such a change in my life and has very definitely changed how I think about my neighbour and God. Praise God!'

STEPPING INTO THE BREACH 24 pages

Claiming the name of Jesus and His blood in personal and intercessory prayer leads to dynamic results.

THE SECRET OF LOVING — WHEN YOU CAN'T 24 pages

Loving others with the love of Christ and winning them over to Him by reflecting His example.

SONGS

GLORY BE TO GOD! 16 pages
Two sets of 31 verses for worship every day of the month.

I WANT TO CONSOLE YOU 72 pages
Songs of Love and Comfort for Our Lord in His Suffering Today.

SONGS AND PRAYERS OF VICTORY 84 pages
– complete with a song cassette –
As Christians we are called to fight the good fight of faith. Many have found this selection of songs and prayers to be a great help in praying for themselves or for others.

SONGS FOR SPIRITUAL WARFARE 48 pages
– complete with a song cassette –
A variety of songs and prayers offering spiritual armament for overthrowing satanic strongholds, freeing captives, cancelling curses and experiencing release from demonic bondage and oppression.